Fat Ducks

Written by Jill Eggleton
Illustrated by Astrid Matijasevic

Rigby

Ducks lived on the beach on Beach Street.
The people at Number One Beach Street said,
"Ducks can't find food in the sand."

And they fed the ducks.

The people at Number Nine
Beach Street said,
"Ducks can't find food
in the sand."
And they fed the ducks.

Mr. Mike at Number Five Beach Street said, "Ducks can't find food in the sand."

And he fed the ducks.

The people on Beach Street **all** fed the ducks.

The ducks got
fatter and fatter.
A dog came to the beach
and chased the ducks.
But the ducks were so fat
they couldn't fly.

They fell over in the sand.
They got sand
in their feathers
and sand in their bills.

Mr. Mike said to the people
on Beach Street,
"Those ducks are too fat.
What can we do?"

"We could take them to the gym," said a woman.

"We can't take ducks to a gym," said Mr. Mike. "The gym is for people."

"We could take them to
a diet class," said a man.

"We can't take ducks
to a diet class," said Mr. Mike.
"A diet class is for people."

"I know," said Mr. Mike. "We could make a schedule to feed the ducks."

Schedule for Feeding the Ducks

Monday — 1 Beach Street
Tuesday — 2 Beach Street
Wednesday — 3 Beach Street
Thursday — 4 Beach Street
Friday — 5 Beach Street

"Who will feed the ducks on Saturday and Sunday?" said the people.

"On Saturday and Sunday, those ducks can feed themselves!" said Mr. Mike.

13

A Schedule

Schedule
for Feeding the Ducks

Monday   1 Beach Street

Tuesday   2 Beach Street

Wednesday   3 Beach Street

Thursday   4 Beach Street

Friday   5 Beach Street

Saturday   Ducks

Sunday   Ducks

Guide Notes

Title: Fat Ducks
Stage: Early (3) – Blue

Genre: Fiction
Approach: Guided Reading
Processes: Thinking Critically, Exploring Language, Processing Information
Written and Visual Focus: Schedule

THINKING CRITICALLY
(sample questions)
- What do you think this story could be about?
- What do you know about ducks? Where do they live? What do they like to eat?
- Look at pages 2 and 3. What do you think the people are feeding the ducks?
- Look at pages 6 and 7. Why do you think the ducks can't fly?
- Look at page 8. What could the people be thinking about?
  How do you think the problem of the fat ducks could be solved?
- What is a schedule?
- Look at page 12. Why do you think it was important to have a schedule?
- Why do you think the people don't want to feed the ducks on Saturday and Sunday?

EXPLORING LANGUAGE

Terminology
Title, cover, illustrations, author, illustrator

Vocabulary
Interest words: schedule, feathers, bills, gym, diet
High-frequency words (new): one, take, themselves, five, those
Positional word: over
Compound words: themselves, Sunday

Print Conventions
Capital letter for sentence beginnings and names (**Mr. M**ike), periods, exclamation marks, quotation marks, commas, question marks